WATER BUFFALO

by Liza Jacobs

BLACKBIRCH®
PRESS

San Diego • Detroit • New York • San Francisco • Cleveland • New Haven, Conn. • Waterville, Maine • London • Munich

© 2003 by Blackbirch Press™. Blackbirch Press™ is an imprint of The Gale Group, Inc., a division of Thomson Learning, Inc.

Blackbirch Press™ and Thomson Learning™ are trademarks used herein under license.

For more information, contact
The Gale Group, Inc.
27500 Drake Rd.
Farmington Hills, MI 48331-3535
Or you can visit our Internet site at http://www.gale.com

Photographs © 1998 by Chang Yi-Wen

Cover Photograph © Corel

© 1998 by Chin-Chin Publications Ltd.

No. 274-1, Sec.1 Ho-Ping E. Rd., Taipei, Taiwan, R.O.C.
Tel: 886-2-2363-3486 Fax: 886-2-2363-6081

LIBRARY OF CONGRESS CATALOGING-IN-PUBLICATION DATA

Jacobs, Liza.
  Water buffalo / by Liza Jacobs.
    v. cm. -- (Wild wild world)
  Includes bibliographical references.
  Contents: Water buffalo -- Water buffalos are plant-eaters -- Water
  buffalo are social animals -- Many kinds.
    ISBN 1-4103-0055-2 (hardback : alk. paper)
    1. Water buffalo--Juvenile literature. [1. Water buffalo.] I. Title.
  II. Series.

    SF401.W34J23 2003
    599.64'2--dc21
                                                                2003001493

Printed in Taiwan
10 9 8 7 6 5 4 3 2 1

Table of Contents

About Water Buffalos

Wild water buffalos live in parts of India, Asia, and Central America. Domestic water buffalos have been trained to live alongside people. They can be found in Europe, Australia, and parts of Africa, South America, and the United States.

Wild buffalo stand 8 to 10 feet tall and weigh between 1,500 to 2,600 pounds! Domestic buffalos are a bit smaller. They often weigh between 550 to 1,200 pounds.

A water buffalo's hide is dark and has a thin covering of hair. Males and females have horns with wrinkled grooves. The horns curve out from the side of the head and around toward the back.

A water buffalo's ears stick out at the sides and are fringed with hair. Buffalo have large nostrils and a keen sense of smell.

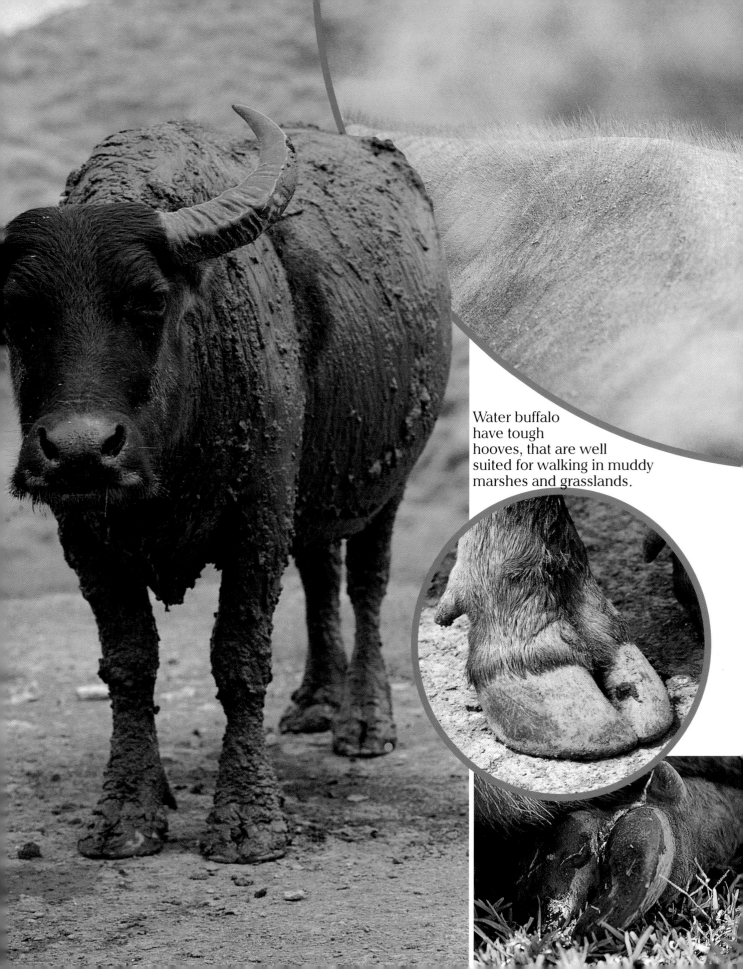

Water buffalo have tough hooves, that are well suited for walking in muddy marshes and grasslands.

Life with Water

Flies and other bugs are constantly buzzing around water buffalo.

The buffalo spend a lot of time bathing and wallowing in mud and water. This helps keep the bugs away.

While they are in the water, it is common to see only a part of a water buffalo's head poking out.

Water buffalo are often caked with a layer of mud. This helps keep insects from biting. They also use their tails to swat bugs away.

Helper Birds

In addition to taking mud baths, water buffalos have some extra help keeping clean.

An ox pecker is a bird often seen on or near a water buffalo.

Ox peckers pick off flies and ticks from a water buffalo and eat them.

In this way, the water buffalo gets rid of pests, the ox pecker gets a good meal, and both animals are happy.

Food and Cud

Water buffalos are plant-eaters. They like grasses, mushrooms, and many other plants that grow in or near water.

Plant foods are made of tough fibers that are hard to digest. Like deer, sheep, goats, and cows, water buffalo have special stomachs that help them digest their food.

When these animals eat, they chew and swallow quickly.

One part of their stomach, the rumen, helps break down the food. This partially chewed food is then brought back up and chewed again. This is called chewing cud. After the cud is swallowed, it can be fully digested.

Social Animals

Water buffalo are social animals. They like to live in groups, or herds.

They often sleep together. Water buffalos will sleep almost anywhere.

Sometimes they sleep standing up. They even sleep in the mud!

Important Horns

Like most cattle, a water buffalo's horns grow as it gets older.

A water buffalo's horns are very important in the wild. They use their horns to defend themselves.

When a buffalo is about to strike an enemy, it lowers its head. This position points the horns at the target. It also lets the other animal know it is about to charge.

Adults can fight off large animals such as rhinoceros with their long, sharp horns.

Bulls, Cows, and Calves

A male water buffalo is called a bull. A female is called a cow.

During mating season, a bull mates with several females.

About 10 months later, a cow will have 1 or 2 babies. Babies are called calves.

Calves drink their mothers' rich milk for 6 to 9 months. Young calves stay close to their mothers.

Helping Humans

Water buffalo are related to cattle, oxen, and other kinds of buffalo.

For thousands of years, many of these animals have been used by humans as work animals in different parts of the world. They plow fields and carry heavy loads. Cattle are also a good source of meat.

The yellow cows on these pages are dairy cattle. Their milk is used to make butter and cheese.

Different Kinds of Buffalo

Water buffalo are related to the African Cape buffalo. The Asian water buffalo and the African Cape buffalo are very similar. In fact, they are often confused as the same animal.

One way to tell them apart is by their horns. The horns of a male cape buffalo go across the top of its head.

Cape buffalos live in Africa, amongst other African animals such as giraffes. They live in large herds on the African grasslands.

Bison Cousins

Water buffalo are also related to the North American buffalo, or bison.

Bison have a large hump above their shoulders. A thick, shaggy coat covers the front of their bodies. The back part is covered with thinner hair. Males often have a black beard.

Like water buffalo, bison are social animals that live in groups. Adult males form one group. Females and young animals stay in another.

Sometimes they join together to hunt for food.

For More Information

Brodsky, Beverly. *Buffalo.* New York: Winslow Press, 2003.

Crewe, Sabrina. *The Buffalo.* Austin, TX: Raintree Steck-Vaughn, 1997.

Glossary

bull a male water buffalo

calf a baby water buffalo

cow a female water buffalo

cud partially chewed food that is brought up to be chewed again